THE FUTURE IS FEMALE

ALTERNATOR BOOKS™

Changemakers in
THE ARTS AND LITERATURE

Women Leading the Way

CROWN SHEPHERD

Lerner Publications ◆ Minneapolis

Lerner Publications Company
An imprint of Lerner Publishing Group, Inc.
241 First Avenue North
Minneapolis, MN 55401 USA

For reading levels and more information, look up this title at www.lernerbooks.com.

Main body text set in Aptifer Sans LT Pro Medium.
Typeface provided by Linotype AG.

Editor: Brianna Kaiser **Designer:** Athena Currier **Photo Editor:** Annie Zheng
Lerner team: Martha Kranes

Library of Congress Cataloging-in-Publication Data

Names: Shepherd, Crown, author.
Title: Changemakers in the arts and literature : women leading the way / Crown Shepherd.
Description: Minneapolis : Lerner Publications, [2024] | Series: The future is female (Alternator books) | Includes bibliographical references and index. | Audience: Ages 8–12 | Audience: Grades 4–6 | Summary: "Whether they are painters, dancers, writers, or photographers, women have made incredible artistic accomplishments. Readers will love learning all about the women making change in the arts and literature"— Provided by publisher.
Identifiers: LCCN 2023010650 (print) | LCCN 2023010651 (ebook) | ISBN 9798765608869 (library binding) | ISBN 9798765625002 (paperback) | ISBN 9798765618509 (epub)
Subjects: LCSH: Women artists—United States—Biography—Juvenile literature. | BISAC: JUVENILE NONFICTION / Biography & Autobiography / Women
Classification: LCC NX511.5 .S54 2024 (print) | LCC NX511.5 (ebook) | DDC 700.82—dc23/eng/20230524

LC record available at https://lccn.loc.gov/2023010650
LC ebook record available at https://lccn.loc.gov/2023010651

Manufactured in the United States of America
1-1009548-51564-6/26/2023

Table of Contents

INTRODUCTION

Making History

In June 2015, Misty Copeland took the stage as the lead role in the American Ballet Theatre's *Swan Lake*. The American Ballet Theatre is one of the top ballet companies in the US. That month Copeland became the first Black principal dancer in the company's history.

At thirteen Copeland started ballet. That's late for most ballet dancers. But her talent and hard work earned her starring roles and led her to worldwide fame.

Misty Copeland rehearses *Swan Lake* with ballet dancer Brooklyn Mack (*left*) in 2015.

From illustrating to writing poetry, women have been breaking barriers in the arts and in literature for thousands of years. Not every great artist and writer can be included in this book. But the ones mentioned here are among those making history and paving the way for other women to make change.

CHAPTER 1

Art Changing the World

Women create many forms of art. From paintings to photos, artists use their work to share cultures and ideas.

Painting Native American History

Joan Hill, also known as Chea-se-quah ("red bird" in Cherokee), painted in several styles. Hill focused her art on Native Americans, including her Creek and Cherokee family history.

Joan Hill with her painting *The Indian Family* in 1974

In 1974 the Five Civilized Tribes Museum honored Hill with a Master Artist award. She was the first woman to receive it. The museum preserves the art and culture of the Cherokee, Chickasaw, Choctaw, Muscogee, and Seminole Nations.

Hill received over 270 awards for her paintings. She is the most recognized female Native American artist.

Sculptures for Change

Maya Lin is an award-winning artist. As a twenty-one-year-old college student, she designed the Vietnam Veterans Memorial in Washington, DC. The memorial honors the US service members that died in the Vietnam War (1955–1975).

Lin also makes large artworks that focus on the environment. In 2021 her work *Ghost Forest* showed in New York City. Lin hopes the artwork will encourage others to act against climate change. The US government awarded Lin the National Medal of Arts in 2009.

Maya Lin displays her final design of the Vietnam Veterans Memorial in 1981.

FINE ART GROUP

The National Association of Women Artists is a fine art group for women in the US. It awards artists, offers art education, and has events where artists show their work.

An event put on by the National Association of Women Artists

Lights, Cameras, Action

When she was twenty-five years old, Patricia Cardoso moved from Colombia to the US to be a filmmaker. She directed the 2002 film *Real Women Have Curves*. It won many awards.

> **"You have to know your strengths and your stretches. It is hard. But if you have persistence and you have patience, you are going to be able to tell your stories."**
>
> —PATRICIA CARDOSO, 2015

In 2019 the film was added to the National Film Registry at the Library of Congress. The registry includes films that have culturally impacted the US. Cardoso is the first female Latinx director of a film added to the registry. Cardoso teaches filmmaking and works to get more women of color to direct films.

Patricia Cardoso attends the 2019 Women in Film Annual Gala.

The Celebrity Photographer

Annie Leibovitz is a legend in the photography world. In 1973 she became the chief photographer of *Rolling Stone*, a magazine with articles on music, politics, and pop culture.

Leibovitz has been photographing celebrities since the early 1980s. She has taken photos of actors, athletes, and singers, including LeBron James, Queen Elizabeth II, and Miley Cyrus. In 1991 Leibovitz became the first female photographer featured at the National Portrait Gallery—a museum with images of famous Americans.

Annie Leibovitz presents her work *Women: New Portraits* in 2016 in Italy.

CHAPTER 2

Life through Illustrations

Women illustrators help give a voice to women from all backgrounds. They use their talent to share ideas and create characters never seen before.

Themes That Readers Understand

Patricia Polacco spent most of her life working on protecting artworks from being damaged. But when she was forty-one years old, she started her writing and illustrating career.

Polacco wrote her first story to help her son understand diabetes, a disease he had. A person with diabetes can't make

A reading of Patricia Polacco's book *Mrs. Katz and Tush* in 2012

enough insulin—a kind of hormone that controls how the body uses sugar. Polacco has illustrated over one hundred books. Her work has won many awards and centers on diversity, acceptance, and community.

G. Willow Wilson attends a Marvel Comics exhibit at the Museum of Pop Culture in 2018.

First Muslim Superhero

G. Willow Wilson converted to Islam in her early twenties after years of studying religion and teaching English in Egypt. A fan of comics since she was a child, Wilson published her first graphic novel, *Cairo*, in 2007.

In 2012 Marvel Comics hired Wilson. She made the Pakistani American character Kamala Khan, also known as Ms. Marvel. Ms. Marvel, the first Muslim superhero, came out in 2014. Wilson's work has been published in over a dozen languages and sold worldwide.

THE ART PRODIGY

Colleen Doran (*below*) has been called an art prodigy ever since winning a Disney art contest when she was five years old. At twelve she began to write and illustrate her comic series *A Distant Soil*. It has sold over five hundred thousand copies worldwide. Doran has illustrated advertisements and comics.

An Illustrating Leader

Vashti Harrison is an author, illustrator, and filmmaker. While studying film in college, she found a love for telling stories.

In 2016 she won an illustrating competition. The day after winning the competition, an art director reached out to Harrison to illustrate a book. Harrison wrote and illustrated her first book, *Little Leaders: Bold Women in Black History*, in 2017. She created it after she had the idea to make a drawing of unsung heroes for every day of Black History Month.

Vashti Harrison speaks about her book *Little Legends: Exceptional Men in Black History* at an event in 2019.

CHAPTER 3

Writing with Purpose

Women write poems, plays, books, and more.
Writers use their words to tell stories that reflect their own lives and the lives of other people.

Important Black Stories
Toni Morrison shaped the world of fiction. She published her first novel, *The Bluest Eye*, in 1970 when she was thirty-nine. Morrison centered her characters and stories on Black culture when most writers were only writing about white characters.

Toni Morrison (*left*) receives the 1993 Nobel Prize in Literature.

Morrison wrote many award-winning books. In 1993 Morrison became the first Black woman to win a Nobel Prize in Literature. The award is given for great achievements in literature.

Memoir Firsts

Janet Mock is a Black and Kānaka Maoli (Native Hawaiian) trans woman. After studying journalism at New York

NOBEL PRIZE IN LITERATURE

Since the first woman, Swedish author Selma Ottilia Lovisa Lagerlöf (*below*), won the Nobel Prize in Literature in 1909, seventeen women have won the award.

University, she worked as a writer and editor for five years. In 2012 she started a movement on social media around the hashtag #girlslikeus. She created it to speak about the violence toward LGBTQIA+ youth.

> **"Being able to control the narrative, shape, and form the way I view my experiences . . . [has] opened the world up for me."**
>
> —JANET MOCK, ABOUT TELLING STORIES OF TRANS WOMEN, 2020

Mock wrote two memoirs about her life as a trans woman. In 2018 she made history by being the first trans woman of color to write and direct for a television show.

Janet Mock talks about one of her books at an event in 2017.

Poetry of the Unseen

At seventeen, Laurie Clements Lambeth was diagnosed with multiple sclerosis (MS). MS is a disease where the immune system attacks the coating on nerves of the brain and spinal cord. Lambeth started writing to better understand her disease and how it relates to the world.

Lambeth has written nonfiction and poetry. Her poetry often focuses on disabilities and diseases that people cannot see. She won the National Poetry Series Award in 2006.

A Broadway Playwright

Young Jean Lee moved from South Korea to the US with her parents when she was two. In high school she was interested in William Shakespeare's plays. She studied English, including the works of Shakespeare, in college.

Lee started her own theater company in 2003

Young Jean Lee in 2018

USING PEN NAMES

Authors sometimes publish their books under a pen name. A pen name is a name an author uses on their books instead of their real name. Some authors publish their books with their initials. Susan Eloise Hinton wrote many books under the name S. E. Hinton. Her 1967 book *The Outsiders* is the best-selling young adult book of all time.

In 2011 Susan Eloise Hinton (*center*) attends an event for the 1983 movie *The Outsiders* with Ralph Macchio (*left*) and Christopher Thomas Howell (*right*), actors from the movie.

called Young Jean Lee's Theater Company. From 2003 to 2016, Lee wrote and directed twelve plays for the company. In 2018 she became the first Asian American woman to have a play on Broadway.

CHAPTER 4

Making Strides in Dance

Women perform all kinds of dance around the world. Through dance, they teach and inspire change in the next generation.

Fighting Racism through Dance

As a young girl, Debbie Allen was denied access to the Houston Ballet School because she was Black. But that didn't stop her. She spent her career as a dancer, actor, and director.

Allen won choreography awards in 1982 and 1983 for her work on the television show *Fame*. In 2001 she opened the

Debbie Allen Dance Academy. Allen wanted to help Black and Latinx communities have access to dance and theater. Dancers from all over the US travel to California to take dance classes with Allen.

Debbie Allen at the Industry Dance Awards in 2018

FAMOUS TAPPER

Michelle Dorrance (*below*) is a world-famous tap dancer, choreographer, and dance teacher. In 2021 Dorrance choreographed her first Broadway musical, *Flying Over Sunset*.

Champion Hoop Dancer

Lisa Odjig is a Wiikwemkoong First Nation member and hoop dancer. She has been hoop dancing since she was sixteen. Hoop dancing is a Native American form of storytelling. The dancer moves the hoops into shapes that represent animals and symbols.

Lisa Odjig performing a hoop dance in 2005

In 2000 Odjig became the first woman to win the Heard Museum World Championship Hoop Dance contest. She is a seven-time winner of the contest and the only woman to have won. She did hoop dancing on the competition show *Canada's Got Talent* in 2012.

YOUNG BALLET DANCER

In 2019 eleven-year-old Charlotte Nebres became the first Black ballet dancer to play Marie in the New York City Ballet *Nutcracker*. The company has performed the ballet each year since 1954.

Dancing on Television

Maddie Ziegler rose to fame at eight years old after being on the show *Dance Moms*. When she was eleven, she starred in singer Sia's music video "Chandelier." In 2016 she became a judge on the dance competition show *So You Think You Can Dance: The Next Generation*.

Ziegler has starred in over a dozen music videos and has danced all over the world for award shows and music festivals. She has written books and has starred in television shows and movies, including the 2021 movie *West Side Story*.

Maddie Ziegler attends the premiere of the 2021 movie *West Side Story*.

CONCLUSION

Future Artists and Writers

Women are using art and literature to change the world. They are building spaces for children to follow their dreams and are opening doors for the next generation of women in the arts and literature. You can be a leader in the arts and literature too!

Copeland and sports journalist Amanda Balionis (*right*) speak at an event in 2022.

Glossary

choreography: a set of steps and movements in dance

climate change: a change in the usual weather conditions of a place

culture: the language, customs, ideas, and art of a group of people

director: a person who guides the making of a movie, television show, or play

disability: a physical or mental condition that makes it more difficult for a person to do certain activities

filmmaker: a person who directs or produces films

illustrator: a person who draws or creates pictures for books, magazines, and more

preserve: to protect or keep safe from loss

principal: a dancer of the highest rank in a dance company

prodigy: a young person with exceptional talent

trans: a person whose gender identity or expression is different from the sex they were assigned at birth

Source Notes

10   Ana Luisa González, "Latina Filmmaker Patricia Cardoso Was Almost Hired to Direct a Feature 7 Times," *LA Weekly*, October 20, 2015, https://www.laweekly.com/latina-filmmaker-patricia-cardoso-was -almost-hired-to-direct-a-feature-7-times/.

20   Jasmine Fox-Suliaman, "Janet Mock: Writing a New Vision for Hollywood," Who What Wear, October 1, 2020, https://www.whowhatwear.com/janet-mock-interview.

Learn More

Britannica Kids: Toni Morrison
https://kids.britannica.com/students/article/Toni-Morrison/312581

CBC Kids: Do You Know What Hoop Dancing Is?
https://www.cbc.ca/kids/articles/do-you-know-what-hoop-dancing-is

Kawa, Katie. *Misty Copeland: Making a Difference as a Dancer.* New York: KidHaven, 2022.

Kiddle: Maddie Ziegler Facts for Kids
https://kids.kiddle.co/Maddie_Ziegler

Maya Lin Studio
https://www.mayalinstudio.com

Nnachi, Ngeri. *Changemakers in Music: Women Leading the Way.* Minneapolis: Lerner Publications, 2024.

Reed, Darcy. *Extraordinary Women with Cameras: 35 Photographers Who Changed How We See the World.* San Rafael, CA: Rocky Nook, 2022.

Smith, Elliott. *Black Achievements in Arts and Literature: Celebrating Gordon Parks, Amanda Gorman, and More.* Minneapolis: Lerner Publications, 2024.

Index

Photo Acknowledgments

Image credits: The Washington Post/Getty Images, p. 5; Tullous, Don, Oklahoma Publishing Company Photography Collection, Courtesy of the Oklahoma Historical Society, 2012.201.B0261.0615, p. 7; Bettmann/Getty Images, p. 8; awa1889/Wikimedia Commons (CC BY-SA 4.0), p. 9; WENN/Alamy, p. 10; Matteo Valle/Stringer/Getty Images Entertainment/Getty Images, p. 11; ZUMA Press/Alamy, p. 13; Jim Bennett/Getty Images Entertainment/Getty Images, p. 14; MayCauseDrowsiness/Wikimedia Commons (CC0 1.0), p. 15; Jim Spellman/Getty Images Entertainment/Getty Images, p. 16; AP Photo, pp. 18, 19; Desiree Navarro/WireImage/Getty Images, p. 20; Walter McBride/WireImage/Getty Images, p. 21; AP Photo/Kelly Kerr, p. 22; Media Punch/Alamy, p. 24; Malcolm Park/Alamy, p. 25; Heinz Ruckemann/Alamy, p. 26; AP Photo/Chris Pizzello, p. 27; Craig Barritt/Stringer/Getty Images Entertainment/Getty Images, p. 29. Design elements: Old Man Stocker/Shutterstock; MPFphotography/Shutterstock; schab/Shutterstock.

Cover: ullstein bild/ullstein bild Premium/Getty Images (Maya Lin); AP Photo/Xavier Collin/Image Press Agency (Maddie Ziegler); Olga Besnard/Shutterstock (Toni Morrison).